"Russo's *Meaning to Go to the Or* dramas of gardening' in a broad chaos, brawling trees, and 'feet cows.' Robins and squirrels punctuate grass in for a substantial p while the compost trails of worms invest the native vegetation. 'It begins with walking,' yet returns to its yard, to register the mucked, embattled, compromised steps of learning from proximity. This poetry sings brightly for the ultra-local, itself a collection and dispersion of sympathies, grasped at earth magnitude. I admire Russo's yard work, as attuned to the 'workaday' as to the squawk of unidentified bird calls, for its self-awareness, humor, and sense of beauty. It's strong yet supple writing: poetry for what's underfoot, in any weather."

—Jonathan Skinner

"Linda Russo has written an exceptional bioregional text—one that re-seeds landscapes with a re-fashioned language of 'interspecies inhabitance.' To go to the root, here, maybe anywhere, is to go into a weaving of multiple strands, to re-order the many layers of displacement, settlement, and development and—finding the remnants of indigenous ecosystems along the bioregional margins—reveal that 'things' are once again 'assemblies,' coherences around which information gathers. Even the incursion of Walmart signals the simultaneous fixity and impermanence of the human element. Testing 'the analytic capacity of sentient poetry,' Russo encourages us to live simultaneously lightly, and with deeper roots. This is exactly what I'd hoped the meeting of poetry and ecology would give us."

—Stephen Collis

"As a sensitive study of living systems, *Meaning to Go to the Origin in Some Way* demonstrates receptivity and attuned openness in astounding, replenishing ways. Russo takes into consideration the complex local ecosystems in which she lives—a local and historical inquiry that involves bodies and languages—a surging bio-semiotics of human-animal relation. Anthropologist Anna Tsing writes, 'human nature is an interspecies relation-ship.' This charged understanding is echoed throughout Russo's polyvalent text that concerns itself most explicitly with 46.7325°N, 117.1717°W": The Confluence, South Fork Palouse River & Paradise Creek, Pullman, WA U.S.A—but also all that pulsates through, within and around. Various modes of presencing and thinking are engaged within this capacious document in an effort to thrive within cultivated, regulated, domesticated and also occasionally almost wild domains—together with the diverse organisms that share these domains and make their meanings known."

—Brenda Iijima

Also by Linda Russo

o going out (chapbook)
Secret Silent Plan (chapbook)
MIRTH
picturing everything closer visible (chapbook)

Linda Russo

*Meaning to Go
to the Origin
in Some Way*

Shearsman Books

First published in the United Kingdom in 2015 by
Shearsman Books
50 Westons Hill Drive
Emersons Green
BRISTOL
BS16 7DF

Shearsman Books Ltd Registered Office
30–31 St. James Place, Mangotsfield, Bristol BS16 9JB
(this address not for correspondence)

www.shearsman.com

ISBN 978-1-84861-393-5

Cover photo collage by the author.
From top right: Rose Creek Preserve; wheat field adjacent to Rose
Creek Preserve; a portion of the bank of the Palouse River (South Fork);
riverwashed "nests" near the Palouse River (South Fork).

Contents

Look around, dear head, you've never read
of the ground that takes you away.

—*Lorine Niedecker*

but none of it 'indigenous' to here except
through conviction of the poet combining

these strands into a useful cord…

—*Joanne Kyger*

Historical Vegetation

Mixed Conifer Woodlands
Grand Fir/White Fir
Interior Douglas-fir
Interior Ponderosa Pine
Shrub or Herb/Tree Regeneration
Big Sagebrush
Agropyron Bunchgrass
Fescue/Bunchgrass
Herbaceous Wetlands
Wetland/Shrub
Water
Urban
Cropland/Hay/Pasture
Exotic Forbs/Annual Grass

Existing Vegetation

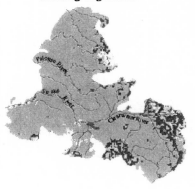

GOING TO SURVEY WALMART CONSTRUCTION
FROM THE CREST OF PIONEER HILL

it begins with walking, feet mucked by competing agendas
and a wish to speak as part and parcel
> *a rare Cow Parsnip community*

part of a history of embattlement
of space being filled
> *a well-preserved remnant of Idaho fescue grasslands*

where walking is merely civil
and walking is compromised
> *still the largest remnant of natural Palouse vegetation*

citizenry

I wish to invoke freely a culture of interspecies inhabitance
> *valuable thickets of Douglas Hawthorne*

conflicts resolved, powers balanced

sometimes it takes less than a minute
> *Magpie Forest, Rose Creek, Smoot Hill*

you hitch up your bird wings hoping

> *This is a ground poem. It takes flight but weighed with
> the gravity of the situation; it wants to see the beauty, and
> it is necessary to witness the beauty; it wants to believe
> that in its acts of spatial reclamation new worlds begin. It
> sets out to be derivative of the sentient world in the only
> human way it knows – to return through animals.*

whereas, a sort of smallness is
whereas, the tentacles of my circumference
whereas, a kind of attending to
whereas, breakdown quietness after moving
whereas, heart + beat =
whereas, I think affects
whereas, endlessly clear and endlessly dirty

whereas, drops the wood deck darkens
whereas, sweeping sensitive and greenly
whereas, flat-footed birdsong intends
whereas, lure of the windex tapestry

Orchard Sprung

if any are uncertain, we show them
    how we map an informal space between us

until a sudden sky reveals
    the mold into which
so much behavior is cast (as so many
       American women know)

when none are near

how many distances do animals have?
  flight distance, critical distance, personal distance

so many she forgets her own locality
in the fixed-feature space of her culture

(the walls don't tell)

together in our unconscious geographies
    I'm nobody you know

but now distance binds us

she said: I want to be the last wild female rabbit
   on sagebrush flats – that farmers hate

     solitary in her territory
  tolerating sagebrush toxins

         cuddly but aggressive
    cute yet angry

   burrowing in the deep soil of the sagebrush flats
winter's pinkish tinge fading to brown

I. One Yard

part of it has to be given
while the rest is a repository
beds overgrown with grass and inviting our little wagers

will we have flies, we have flies
whether or not will we have flies

beetles, gnats, fireflies, centipedes
    and a rarely visible mouse

some clay, intensely dirty years, perennial eyes yet no reply

with our experimental modern improvements
coiling into the local geography

we've got our houses to keep
us company

An Essential Radish (on the Pacific Flyway)

simply an essential radish (from "radical" / having roots,
meaning to go to the origin in some way –

on the Pacific Flyway
the seed you planted sprouted, the Least Terns took wing
flashed silhouettes of shorebird (running, pecking)
at Koppel Farm, in landlocked Pullman, June two thousand
                                                    and ten

meaning to go to the origin in some way
          acting animal-like toward boundaries, breathing

Interlacing Words and Things

To turn a place into a field
       interlace words and things
question not & bend the site
       intuit infinite things

to turn a place into a yard
       intuit infinite things
live among rambles, spittle weeds
       the workaday rhythm of wings

to turn a place into a garden
       the workaday rhythm of wings
trills and sheen, sparrows and earwigs
       colorful battles in stings

greenness surges the circulation
       colorful battles in stings
all the stink of thine simplicity
       interlace words and things

lush entangled vines forever theregoing

II. Winter

our yard, though partly grown and hardly deep
gets attention
and it is surprising

(the juices of the grass)

covered with, dappled with, snow
keeping tree trunks, think tree trunks
spiky, true crystals
of an appealing architecture

one advantage in our yard
is learning to love the seldom disagreeable wind

GOING TO SURVEY WALMART CONSTRUCTION
FROM THE CREST OF PIONEER HILL

I am searching for the winding path
in this patch, that patch, this patch, that patch of "land"
crowded and crabbed by the abstraction of space
and powerless to exercise options

> you and I – we comply
> to our contract, extending and retracting
> curling up our edges
> with a gentle hello

(the malady of isolated movement)

I wish to invoke the analytic capacity of sentient poetry

> sit for a spell in my space
> & drink this tea with me

> recall current taxonomies

> it's where you might go
> to reinvest in the blue of Chickory
> or Wormseed Mustard, or Whitlow Grass, or
> Niedeckerweed

patching together remnants, restoring
wild handwork culture

then she said: I think they make too much of dinosaurs

    shopping centers and cheap food production
    the song of arable, of dams, of more
    natives squeezed out in
    the production of more
    arable land

  err-able, likely to err we are

PARTICIPANT AS BIRDS

participant as birds – unlashing from the clouds
    peeking, gauzy and heavily

her small body (there)
    practiced on bird-scales
returns public space
    to public use

    till syllables unlink
    till traffics return

brought back to the familiar, the creaturely
    (existence plus alphabets)

III. Sky

floors of heavy cloud in any shape they please, blown by
electric currents at the horizon

from wells of brick see the air up there   spreading in slaty shadow
cutting across the park, catching a glimpse of blue
opening imaginary lungs so constantly

as we see a mountain in the distance we doubtless follow its lines
surprised when at sunset red lights play over a faded web

(a cohesive social force – skyward poetry)

THE SECRET LIFE OF PLANTS (A CENTO)

the slightest surges of human emotion
hot and perennially in your hands
each attuned to the other

to the animal life that surrounds
even in a shredded leaf
and (in) its redistributed chaos

we discover rituals of real longing and communication
and monitor them independently
(if at all)

IV. Spring

because of delays and damages
we pull down magazines on gardening
encroaching on the space
like reformists, all spiky and weeding

you have only to whistle before they are eaten
and pine and shrink into the earth
as nothing else we want

        grubs and bugs, repellent   (sun and air and rain)

rainbow-green as these new things –
designs twice as sorry

she said: I think you also care
        because you have walked in her paths

        sagebrush, sage grouse
            grasses and forbs
        sage sparrows and Washington ground squirrels
        forbs, the flowers of the grasslands

    "last little rabbit – her confusion & loneliness"

            her worn-out angry eyes

Dear Koppel Farm Gardeners,

Just a word of encouragement. The weeds can be daunting this time of year – growing madly and entangling young sprouts and seedlings. But, take heart – your garden can survive!

The weeds are definitely worse in the early part of the summer when it first warms up. If you can take them in stride and beat back a part of them each weekend, your vegetables will flourish. The weeds calm down as the weather gets hotter and don't take nearly as much effort to control.

You'll never get all of the bindweed/morning glory out (roots can go down over 20 feet), so it works to just pull them up to get rid of the tops. The quack grass is best dug up and removed roots and all. Thistles keep coming back too, but can be chopped with a hoe – as can the lesser evil weeds.

Hang in there – bit by bit – it's worth it!

Koppel Garden Board

V. Summer

among the baking bricks and blistering asphalt
drink, toil, grumble, and die, and all that
    and look down at the lush anxiety of greenery, yes
like victims without work

buy your flowers and after try the thrifty weed
    I will leave my brains in the briar
whack them, it doesn't matter

insects take most of our time

GOING TO SURVEY WALMART CONSTRUCTION
FROM THE CREST OF PIONEER HILL

we in our many vectors crisscross this space
pinned to each other with our kind human greeting
our open, generous, uncomplicated
beg for release
into an imagined space uncompromisingly ours alone
the pearless pear tree and what you learn by proximity
without which we implode

    repetition don't forget   zigzag little ant
        wave wave bunchgrass clovers   wave
      lawngrass, fence & sky   wave   lawngrass, fence & sky

a little rhyme here:

and now a little song:

Song for the Local

Garden to fork, fork to flesh
>   *local-scale crying, thinning the sprouts*
>   *local-scale, local-scale, local-scale crying*

Carbon footprint nitrogen fix
>   local-scale crying, thinning the sprouts
>   local-scale, local-scale, local-scale crying

Resistant to Round-Up, leaving the weeds
>   *local-scale crying, thinning the sprouts*
>   *local-scale, local-scale, local-scale crying*

Knowing, not-knowing a meadow once was
>   *thinning the, thinning the, thinning the sprouts*
>   *local-scale, local-scale, local-scale crying*

VI. City and Country Life

I do not live here because I want to, but because
being free is a kind of sympathy.

> Americans are growing afraid of rural life and crowding
> and claiming privileges that we must associate with
> the calmly artificial politics we call society.

Only in the country can I say this with a certain smartness
though doubtable (meditating in clatter).

Memorizing text as a cure for distress, or flinging oneself
at the landscape. The saddest part. Do not ask for crowding.

If you are interested in restoring native Palouse Prairie vegetation on your land, you have a fascinating challenge in store.

it can be very rewarding –
    the silhouettes of typical vegetation

but it is also tricky to grow;
discuss your particulars with someone
before you begin

        and so we read

                I sew –

                        & sow

                we write

then she said: is cuddly a physical quality?

or emotional receptivity?

the isolated population becomes genetically bottlenecked

Captivity & Morning Kale

"we" are going to solve "nature's" problems

      a little walk in the a.m., take me
      a little walk in the a.m., we shall
      a little, little walk in the a.m., now get to bed

VII. Flowers and Insects

some object of natural interest
in a shady corner of my yard
music in it, in the shade corner of our yard
turning into wild permanence

royal purple throated with gold
and fooled

the freak branches always drew my eye
managing change as I keep my personality:
pulling it out, cropping its shoots, assured

there's always time for that

SOWING

I'd have to
embrace space
through acts
of gardening
so "give me a job"
not bombing or
"getting bombed"
but getting high
on "high grass"
hiding a renegade
zucchini patch
it's a job to recover
space, recover waste
(even in imagination)
"by private woods," or no
it's almost giving
birth (*to a lawnmower!* –
"one of the babies
I'd have") or "getting so"
when you see "waste"
you'd "like to mow"
to downsize to the local
cycles you'd like
to sow

Dark Brown, Friable, Earthy

within one month, his compost, having never been subjected
either to grinding or screening
became a fine, dark brown, friable, earthy material

through whole plateaus or tepid shades and a dimming pulse –

greenness, not a character, or even a characteristic
but a condition
exists
in the grass beneath the leaves
red yellow orange
raining wet leaves

flies caught in a waft, a mulchy flat sweet updraft
greens melding into browns

watch the lettuce leaf passing through one life stage to another
on my plate

GOING TO SURVEY WALMART CONSTRUCTION
FROM THE CREST OF PIONEER HILL

my life by the side yard, driveway, a retail imitation of land use

the songs to sing come happily about the living, us among them

the pearless pear tree and what you learn by proximity

woodpecker on the same telephone pole, same rhythm

at the same time again today

disappointment when "thunder" is the rolling

of a garbage bin

VIII. Autumn

the yard partly bright and brassy, no tapestry, is passing –

the populace is improving
with commercial merchandise picked up for a song
        (in a botany box you never show me, that never appeared)

the dark green of undergrowth is startling
every tree brawling resplendently

after the first experimental batch we jammed them deep and rippling

        one morning, to our distress, they detect our fallacies

    exhibiting dumb surprise

winding pathways & small totems

"Danger BEES"

a small shelter of bent wispy branches hidden in the woods

a 6-stone cairn

the ferocious squirrel I tried to commune with

the bright brickred wood of Pacific Madrone

all the trifling incidents

PACIFIC MADRONE

crooked, irregular branches, brickred bark

take a notebook up to the ridge

highly sensitive, clannish, prone to sickness

will the clouds ever relent

close to the beach, sunny southern exposure

likes to be left alone

for it gathers one's self around one to walk alone in the wood

can't compete with humans

likes to be left alone

IN ORDINARY LANDSCAPES

the aesthetics of industrial agribusiness –
seemingly endless available space –

rubber bark mulch and careful border plantings
around the new bungalow-style houses

thrown up next to acres of wheat – thousands
of acres for export to Japan

more to see over the next hill, too –
the next hill so seldom seen

except by coyote, hawk and deer –
at the Rose Creek Preserve

on an untrodden path
through riotous native grasses

I lay my notebook down, lay down
a sensual geography

approaching the edge where
cultivation cuts a clean line –

a doe in the middle distance
placing hooves across the newly shorn field

of perpetual conflict, of values operating
in the landscape – the withdrawal

of slowly recharging water deposits
from an imperiled aquifer –

an 18-hole golf course that fits
a sustainability plan –

the cemetery's westward-facing slope
with its new view of delivery bays and dumpsters –

a renegade squash patch rooting
the edge space of the community garden –

dirty striped t-shirt, empty bottles, an abandoned
ripped backpack in the grassy tamped-down bed

beneath Pacific Willows that edge the river –
the county dump's table for household toxics exchange –

ecology's sociality traced in the
crisscrossing of domestic thresholds –

the current state of development –
making poem-level decisions that constitute

place in the landscape of the poem –
wildly clipped or abandoned

the social clutter abutting yards breed –
a sense of privacy maintained

in shrinking distances –
the pathways of gossip and news

cut so casually across the grass they leave
no mark, essential pre-conditions of being

in the world alongside other animal byways –
ants secretly conveying a path to the house

along the overgrown ivy, worms unfurling
a fertile compost trail, squirrels crisscrossing

branches, wires, the top of the house
again to the other other side noisily

will you not think me silly for sounding
the ORGANIC MILK ALARM?

or the trees hovering acquiescence against
our perpetual will to crowd?

IX. Everything Now

in spite of our habit of describing
(as widening circles spread in the water)
some forget

so they watch the cities
to shut out the woods
(the woods we can't live without)
they look for corners wooded in their manner, impressed

a container garden – and other works of this kind

drawing life from your soil like a parasite as
the repose of water features
(babbling and strife)
softens the details

tries to give us accidental substance

she said: it's difficult not to get attached

       Titon died, Minnie died, then Wazzu, a death nearly
                  nearly every day, sometimes two;
     Bryn, Ludlow, Mossy, Cara, Piper, Plum, and Onyx

trampled burrows & other insults
  (coyotes, foxes, badgers, owls)

GOING TO SURVEY WALMART CONSTRUCTION FROM THE CREST OF PIONEER HILL

the populace is improving
with commercial merchandise picked up for a song

    and some of us animals out here do live in the
    (prairie, ocean, desert) besides

Palouse Places

Magpie Forest, Rose Creek, Smoot Hill

one of the last remnants of native Palouse shrub-steppe vegetation

valuable thickets of Douglas Hawthorne

a rare Cow Parsnip community

a well-preserved remnant of Idaho fescue grasslands

still the largest remnant of natural Palouse vegetation

Weeds

the sun today, the chimes kick in with the local
accompaniment of (I'm guessing) sparrow
marked/unmarked by conditions, placement

*

Q: does a garden have an audience
A: yes

*

community garden as social solution

*

"read / of the ground" to write (L.N.)

*

property is an abstraction
I'm trying to recover from

*

how did I become so overwhelmed by the things I was discovering?
hoe'd dirt today

*

and warble answered by neighbor

*

10 x 10 foot plot: too small for a roto-tiller but large enough for
a backache

*

almost full moon thinking of you / noble placement some night /
currency of ideas

*

the poem can only partly (re)construct – language also comes to
never entirely from a place

*

looking at boughs then
   tree   tree   tree

*

"the end of the [   ] / is the borders / of my being"

*

who are we to judge the bees
my room is a mess

*

a "green business model" in place of a habitat

*

Jana: "I finally stopped fighting the local soil."

*

Because it smells great here. Oil rigs for pea-vines; garlic
coming up

*

Arrested under the law of Lawn & Garden. Isolated ecologies.

*

or the starlight on the porch since when

*

GREEN GRASS: the most sheltered area, the best fertilized

*

enveloping, beckoning, spread out

*

winding paths (a sort of manifesto)

Always Underfoot

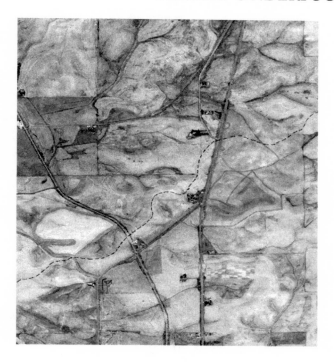

There is no sort of experience that works so constantly and subtly upon man as his regional environment. It orders and determines all the direct, practical ways of his getting up and lying down, of staying in and going out, of housing and clothing and food-getting; it arranges by its progressions of seed times and harvest… It is the thing always before his eye, always at his ear, always underfoot.

Mary Austin

…they never took to the way of writing. Look at their fields, and imagine what they might write, if ever they should put pen to paper. Or what have they not written on the face of the earth already, clearing, and burning, and scratching, and harrowing, and plowing, and subsoiling, in and in, and out and out, and over and over, again and again, erasing what they had already written for want of parchment.

H.D. Thoreau

I. Imaginative Geographical Evidence (1)

*Talk a walk. Write a poem piecing together geographical evidence.
Take another walk. Keep writing a poem. Write imaginative
memory. Send out signals and write the shapes that return. This
is your walk. Keep writing the poem piecing together geographical
evidence and imaginative memory.*

this walk in the mapped omissions:
a rough grassy stretch – a footpath etched deeply diagonally
    transecting
the rough grass unruffled, the curves of a railroad track
of flowing roads, of paths – "Pullman River Walk"
"F.J. Koppel's Milky-Way Dairy" – footpaths cut through trees,
    fields
footpaths down to the riverbank – crossing the river
the unidentified paths along the water where lives are lived
where all feet furthermore
write collaborative geographies

with the satellite image in your head:
the almost perfectly regular white dashes
of "Campus Vista" mobile home park
its relatively fat bands of trees
houses on the ridge above; the etched garden plot grid
of Koppel Community Garden below
white squares of picnic shelter, shed
and west of the Chevron Sunset Mart the field
like a wing broken off, hanging
from a paved spine
where a nearly non-visible winding waterway cleaves
wing and park, wing and garden
where the footbridge bridges

beneath your feet is the landscape rewritten
(physical underfoot realities)
in scars

II. *Geography* / the graphed up geo-

Settlement – shrinking the margins – we revise the already-being-written, a rolling hillside, a spot of prairie, a patch of woods.

We write ourselves in an imagined Euclidean blank, a stable canvas / until houses slide down hillsides, houses that always inch closer to some sea. Inland, sinkholes open and swallow people, houses, cows. The little fictions geologic instability transects.

> *a geographic sense of time is vast, sees*
> *disasters for features, a landscape full of mistakes*
>
> *getting along or healing*
> *our feet hammering the paved footpath*
>
> *physical underfoot realities*
> *sequent occupants, systems and settlements – revealing*
>
> *a history of follies and collapses*

The wind blows across the landscape's features. Human bodies meet little friction, guided across a stretch of parking lot, through wide aisles, through profit, exchange, and loss. At the edge of the asphalt a plastic bag billows up, snagged in tall bunchgrass yellowed in the sun.

III. Map (Community Gardens)

overturn, to dig up to plant to garden
repeating our infinitely small gestures

that move us through and put us in a place
modifying erasing remarking difference

a footbridge is built a footpath extended
"naturewalking" the "industrial" part of the landscape

the remnants of prairie abut the wheatfields
history as cultivated, grasses as relics

the aspen grows, labeled, is history (is what we preserve)
where we mark paths

while the past is where we walked formerly
reformulating survivalist knowledge

IV. Map/Unmap (River)

snows melt, water runs broad on the shallow banks, then
after some spring the water level descends –
someone puts out the plank footbridge removed
late fall (its omission from street maps marks it
as natural) the waterwild noisiness marks it
as natural, the inconsistency, the pleasures, swinging
little sparrow chirps scattered far away and near, glint of sun
on a single glint of a moving windshield too far to hear
long weatherwashed grasses hang off low-hanging branches
dipping in the rumpled surface of swift roiling water

    omitting the name of the river from the map
    *counter*cartography, *not* where we car to

    clusters of Cottonwood line the banks, the riverbed
    their roots dig down several feet below

    the slender stems, their branches
    are not incidental, not flawless, the ten thousand things

    the pattern is a kind of necessity
    clustered instructions

    oh, it's clouding over now, getting cold and
    the Cottonwood may be a Pacific Willow

named road next to
nameless river
map dialectic of depicting
and effacing

    walking/knowing/sensing what is written, the scale of it

V. Collaborative Geography

sometimes something is always changing
other places some things are always staying the same

the same something is painted, some scraping
reveals an archaeology

something is shoveled and something is planted
a hole is dug a few feet deep, a metal pole planted

the boys their feet inscribe the dirt and the grass
the white lines of baseball diamond, later redrawn

ritual of tracing familiar curves and lines
and again the stories of boyhood rewritten

the speed of change and our acts of misreading
history (is and is hidden) there

(mis)readings that make us go (inscribing our paths)
propelling us into a future

so many broken wings on the side
of the road

VI. River Mapping

long weatherwashed grasses dressing the riverbank, wrapping
in and out and around the many-bunched trunks of Pacific
    Willow
stitching in bits of plastic and rag and writing us into its history

a small uncapitalized river in its seasons, writing its place over
    and over –
apples and pears dropping, ripening
and rot and ants and slugs and beetles and
robins and squirrels punctuating the grass
sketching the bark   indigenous writing   resilient rivering –

+

the scale grows slowly manageable
cells, limbs, veins reorganize, other priorities emerge

on-site, thinking

South Fork Palouse River
& Paradise Creek: The Confluence
46.7325° N, 117.1717° W
Pullman, WA. U.S.A

1) muse grasses quiver & brown grasses breeze, 2) flickers of white on water velocities meeting, 3) drifting & churning, suds on water, 4) missing footbridge no walking here, 5) quick water, 6) slow water, 7) sparrow whisper chirps, 8) & wind perking up yells, 9) & the sound of a passing (car), 10) rusty honk of Pheasant, 11) & inconsistent Magpie layered in, 12) single glint of windshield afar, 13) floodplain grasses rapt like nests around the multiple trunks of Cottonwood, 14) & flood grass blossoms, 15) damp green brown dirt paths, 16) & cables forming a skyward brim, slicing it, 17) & taut green grasses poking through flattened beige stalks (waterswept), 18) chirps a few pine trees, 19) roto-tiller ribboning out (intermittent windstreams), 20) small plane demarcates an upper boundary erased (called sky), 21) glint of sun (on water), 22) shadow of strands of hair whipping about on thigh, 23) & wind cool to the cheek, 24) swinging little chirps scattered far away, 25) unexpected embroidered mews (cat or bird or motor), 26) grasses hanging off low hanging branches dipping in swift water, 27) Robin in the path still, 28) flash of Magpie's white wings, 29) Chickadee announced (the verdant green leaves), 30) Crow spreading low little speckles, ants, dirt on pants, 31) little scattered quick water far away ribboning out (between windstreams) slow water walking here, low frequencies dipping in swift water (of confluence)

VII. Imaginative Geographical Evidence (2)

these feet set down in stories, the older geographies:
cows in the common [1870?] grazing bunchgrass, little sunflower,
    silky lupin
physical realities under the slow solid heavy weight of cows
the sound of grass ripping, jaws pulverizing, grinding solid slowly
    moving
roving and eroding morning and evening
patterns – the narrow neck near the [1940?] barn
the flaring shape of the field between the riverbank
and hillside, how many cows, out how far spread
hooves brushing grass, flies in small scatters, urine soaking down
the patterns of scatter, manure, the shifting patterns
of flies and frogs in the river, dirt, rocks, and grasses and water

soil memory, grass memory pushed down through soil seeking
soil remembering, pushed aside, different roots
remembering the exchange of nitrogen
how it moved in the textures of [1950?] prairie
water, temperature, implements, additives and seeds
microbes and roots and beetles and heaviness and soils
the growth patterns of trees along waterways, up hillsides

ten-wide, twelve-wide, and single-wide [1960] home-making
[1970] SE Professional Mall Boulevard

scattered stands of bitter cherry, mountain ash, serviceberry,
plum, hawthorn, alder, water birch, quaking aspen, pacific
willow, juniper, douglas fir, spruce, larch, pine –

a half-inch blanket of [1980] volcanic ash
the first scratchings of plots [1988?] to grid a community garden

apple blossoms clustered on short, spur-like branches
dirt beneath hooves and the heaviness of cows
becoming history

VIII. Physical Underfoot Realities

circumstance brings us to question abridging circumstance
that is, a workaday fact
feet set down in the ruminant patterns of cows
feet trailing along the dirt path by the river
tracing the trailing of feet upon feet, writing
in the shadows of patterns, the whiff of time run-off
that sends one back, wandering, dirt word in hand
returning it

Daynotes on Fields & Forms
(*Flittings*)

quiet gray afternoon tastes green
after tea, after cracking Oklahoma pecan
for northwest red squirrels, after trying to
identify my memory
of a bird (in a bird guide) before more return
"all the trifling incidents"
(Susan Fenimore Cooper, *Rural Hours*)

Sunday Feb. 14

continuous cascade of bird
what could be more natural than
wind stirring the chimes or the sun
stirring birds to cascade, or is it song, or calls
or what they call it, not really song but a
subtle rustling of here   and there
the flat weave of tires
myriad small creatures
the continuous life of cars (on Main and Grand)
in whose time do we breathe now

Sunday Feb. 21

don't forget the sky, or what's at hand

pears, apples, plums and nuts
feed birds, rabbits, worms, beetles etc., squirrels
in the next yard, too

sky brightens
illuminating on the table Columbian cuties winter fruit

March 1 59° poem

it's too cold to go in the yard
dogs bark, the sunlight is doing what?
it's lighting. they are sunning.
it's a luminous hot spot I know little of—
much of the yard is shaded at this hour

3/5, Fri

you're twirling in song or chipping, or cawing are we
speaking the same language your flat note of
inattention what brings us to this place? your see saw
your caw, your hum, scribble, your chip, your wall
of branches, you goddam three dogs barking at it all

*

what writing is indigenous to a place?
The birds punctuating the grass, perhaps
the squirrel punctuating the branch

*

all is awake in its own drama
announcing my folly in this
thing for "my yard"
though it's good to see
you green things I tended last spring
sprouting

a problem. a lesson. to wait

3/6 Sat

bring your pail
and name my flowers
walk with me to till the end of my space
mow my waste (or teach me how)

Sunday, April 18

flight call is a sharp, distinctive plick
what is happiness?
driven out into the rain, not an ordinary rain
but the rain of unselfconsciousness
studded with letters of introduction

I am thus connected, a human right or rite
of many centuries, a spectacle
which seems to be in conflict

the call is a short crisp chip rich with possibility

I react to people one way
but I could react that way

*

    follow the guidelines of garden and yard
    amongst the things and energies of the world
    (some lovely colorful stacks of books)
    we always knew poetic form as a kind of geography

    these small birds, while at hand, not altogether mundane
    white and black and yellow, one brightly so
    in branches

    this is my adventure as a person, anticipating
    leaving and returning, flitting

    5/6 Thurs.

sun beaming off the page, and the subtle smell of lilacs;
warming up the day with a goldfinch

problem is, I don't know if that's a weed

quail in the front yard today, a pair, and then on the roof of the
sunroom I think when I opened the door

do they squak? sqawk? squawk? skwak? squack?

squirrel prefers to cart off hazelnuts (two—leaving one behind);
likes banana, but not strawberry nubs

a little chilly today when sun behind cloud and not too bright,
and now it's slightly drizzling

Saturday 5/8

> where "outside" begins
> experience enhances—multicolored leaves
> shower your head—experience exfoliates
>
> where home ends—it's a common misperception

*

yard looks very different than when last I wrote. Like that bush
covered with yellow flowers that look like daffodils and the
breezy stand of paperwhites.

A background happiness in labor. It feels cold here.

Should I make the rolls or eat the soup and what should I do
tomorrow?

BP's trying to collect oil from the gulf and burning off natural gas, plugging up holes with mud, drilling relief wells for months. Our will in the twenty five-mile radius slick, in the demand for streaming video. Looking out for hummingbirds. 100,000 barrels or 500,000? What's more important – moment with sky? a poem? the downswell in the darkening seawater.

5/18/10 Tuesday

> in a shock of Saturday silence
>
> I could go pull weeds
>
> and I did
>
> and planted
>
> *7/25*

yard aswarm with aphids
        no poem follows from these lines

*

airing my head with the minor distractions of birds—

wind in leaves breathe

the distant machinery of capital

Wednesday 7/28

> Sitting in yellow Adirondack dappled with water from last night's rain – on hummingbird lookout

ran into Aaron on his run

harvested radish sprouts and the zukes are going nuts

Thursday July 29

morning sitting & deciding which book to bring
greeny corner of peach room waking solace

choose books, save things to disk

only have to sit still and think, mind moves—save things to
disk

thunder + rain + sirens last night, this morning
the muted dramas of gardening

Friday July 30

carillon bells – instant uplift

four large birds incredibly high
low, distant-sounding crickets
in a glance distant birds vanish
six birds reappear

hammering, traffic, resonant resident

watch the yard why not
pick pears plums
slice salad pears, pudding perhaps
hear them falling

*

sitting in the yard, a kind of invitation, thought
warm on neck skin breathe skin be porous
perch   limb   listen
for pear drop trees absorb, grass
in an early poem, too much perhaps, what was wrong with that
          poem
sun diagnosis, breath diagnosis
much work to do still, much or more or heavy
a slender branch weighed with tiny plums, birds disperse
widely across the sky, how they disappear

what do we learn from how we see them or hear
squack and hammer and dog yippy dog or hiccup then hush
sand-colored dirt and pink chairs, golden hairs, so much of a
      repetition

*

      help me decide, divine it in me with your dousing stick
      shall I go or no, how shall I live my life, this
      collection and dispersion of energy

      the first little bird peeps arrive

*

who is the "I" that loves "my" yard
trying to live a good life, that's my rule

by *my* I mean all that accompanies

*

who hop and who spread and what do you like to talk about?
knowing grasses, knowing contentment
what there is to be worried about one page later still

crickets then cars   the hums

9/12 Monday, Later

like mobile weeds sometimes
birds chatter in the yard
growing awareness almost time for lunch
sunwarmed distant visual vibrato of leaves
bird song, bird saw
left weedy

*

it's not that my displeasure with Walmart grows any as the
building progresses but the building itself manifests my
disdain as it ruins, outscales, complicates the simple line of
the landscape, obscures the irregular rows of headstones I
can see from the crest of Pioneer Hill, directs me with its
new traffic light, shall it ever sink in

Tues. Sept. 21

Notes, Quotes, Sources & Acknowledgements

"Look around, dear head…" – *New Goose*

"but none of it 'indigenous' …" – "The Fog is halfway over the mesa"

image, p. 8: "Historical Vegetation/Existing Vegetation" from A.E. Black, E. Strand, P. Morgan, J. M. Scott, R. G. Wright, C. Watson, 'Biodiversity and land-use history of the Palouse Bioregion: Pre-European to Present' (1998). In T.D. Sisk, editor. *Perspectives on the Land Use History of North America: A Context for Understanding Our Changing Environment.* Biological Science Report USGS/BRD/BSR-1998-0003 (Revised September 1999). Courtesy of U.S. Geographical Survey. Full color image available at www.palouseprairie.org/display.

"GOING TO SURVEY WALMART CONSTRUCTION FROM THE CREST OF PIONEER HILL / it begins with walking, feet mucked by competing agendas" – 'Walking' by H.D. Thoreau.

"Orchard Sprung" – *The Hidden Dimension* by Edward T. Hall, *Why Different* by Luce Irigaray, *The Complete Poems of Emily Dickinson*, ed. Thomas H. Johnson.

"she said:" & "then she said:"– Titon, Minnie, Wazzu, Bryn, Ludlow, Mossy, Cara, Piper, Plum, and Onyx were rabbits in Washington State University's captive breeding program in the Department of Natural Research Sciences. Thanks to Sarah McCusker for sharing this information.

Poems I-IX ("Yard Works") – *Nature in a City Yard* by Charles M. Skinner.

"Interlacing Words and Things" – *Interlacing Words and Things*, ed. Stephen Bann.

"GOING TO SURVEY WALMART CONSTRUCTION FROM THE CREST OF PIONEER HILL / I am searching for the winding path"– "Niedeckerweed" is "Neckweed" tweaked. The last two lines make reference to Gary Snyder's 'The Rediscovery of Turtle Island': "To work on behalf of the wild is to restore culture."

"PARTICIPANT AS BIRDS" – *The Complete Poems of Emily Dickinson*, ed. Thomas H. Johnson.

"THE SECRET LIFE OF PLANTS (A CENTO)" – *The Secret Life of Plants* by Peter Tompkins.

"Dear Koppel Farm Gardeners" – email, June 22, 2011 (written by Tim Paulitz & included with his permission).

"If you are interested..." from 'The Palouse Prairie.' www.palouseprairie. org. Palouse Prairie Foundation, Moscow, ID, 2002. Courtesy of Palouse Prairie Foundation.

image, p. 29: from R. Daubenmire, 1970. 'Steppe vegetation of Washington.' *Technical Bulletin* 62. Pullman, WA: Washington State University, College of Agriculture, Washington Agricultural Experiment Station.

"Sowing" – "A lawnmower's one of the babies I'd have," Lorine Niedecker, *New Goose*.

"Dark Brown, Friable, Earthy" – *The Secret Life of Plants* by Peter Tompkins.

"Danger BEES" – "all the trifling incidents," Susan Fenimore Cooper, *Rural Hours*.

"IN ORDINARY LANDSCAPES" – "To be part of a landscape, to derive our identity from it, is an essential pre-condition of our being-in-the-world" – J.B. Jackson, *Landscape in Sight: Looking at America;* "field of perpetual conflict" – J.B. Jackson, *Discovering the Vernacular Landscape*.

"WEEDS" – "read / of the ground" – Lorine Niedecker, *New Goose*; "the end of the world / is the borders / of my being" – Charles Olson, *The Maximus Poems*.

"ALWAYS UNDERFOOT" – "And if identities, both specifically spatial and otherwise, are indeed constructed relationally then that poses the question of the geography of those relations of construction. It raises questions of the politics of those geographies and our relationship to and responsibility for them; and it raises, conversely and perhaps less expectedly, the potential geographies of our social responsibility." – Doreen Massey, *For Space*.

image p. 51: Soil Conservation Plan Map (aerial photograph, detail). Verle G. Kaiser Papers. Courtesy of Manuscripts, Archives, and Special Collections, Washington State University.

"There is no sort of experience..." – 'Regionalism and American Fiction.'

"...they never took..." – *A Week on the Concord and Merrimack Rivers*.

'South Fork Palouse River / & Paradise Creek: The Confluence / 46.7325°N, 117.1717°W / Pullman, WA, U.S.A.' Googlemaps image.

"VII: Imaginative Geographical Evidence (2)" – SE Professional Mall Boulevard: *SE Koppel Farm Community Garden Road, in a future imagined geography.*

§

Over six years ago, I resettled in the Palouse bioregion of eastern Washington, a land like none I had known, with gorgeous undulating hills of wheat that shift like a green animal pelt in the summer breeze as far as the eye can see, laid out in the patterns of large-scale agricultural production. Within, this landscape, many small biomes – orchards, retired orchard-forests and other stands of trees, native prairie, buttes, farming homesteads active and defunct, riparian zones, ball parks, cemeteries, community gardens, strip malls, big box stores, parking lots, main streets, suburban yards – cluster here and there. Poetry, as a form of human attention, helped me make a home in this place, and I would like to thank many individuals who accompanied the writing of this work, taking place-writing workshops with me, or walking and thinking along in other ways: Rebecca Goodrich, Patricia Hine, Cameron Hoey, Hallie Kaiser, Rachel Clark, Kirk McAuley, Craig Morris, Matthew O'Malley, Edie-Marie Roper, Jean Russo, Nicole Russo, and Kaia Sand. I would also like to thank the editors of the following publications in which several of these poems appeared: *Capitalism Nature Socialism, Fact-Simile, Horse Less Review, Interim, Shearsman, Spiral Orb, Summer Stock, The Goose, Tinfish*. Eric Magrane, as co-curator of 'Curating the Cosmos' (http://cargocollective.com/curatingthecosmos), included a photodocumentary essay on some of the groundwork for this book, and for this I thank him. Several of these poems were written during an Artist Residency at Centrum in Port Townsend, Washington. Several more of these poems were written as self-appointed poet-in-residence at Pullman Community Garden at Koppel Farm.

This book is dedicated to all beings in all places.

§

A Note on Methodology

In a landscape, walking is a form of reading, an immersive whole-body translation of and into what's there, the give and resistance of it against the soles and the pores, the wind as it moves across the landscape's features of which you are now a part along with the small rattling leaf sounds of other animalkind. Through poetic inquiries – "seeing" with the "worn-out angry eyes" of the last Columbia River Basin Pygmy Rabbit, countermapping terrain portrayed in satellite imagery, re-imagining histories and geographies, on-site writing and reading along with squirrels and terns and snakes and sparrows and flickers – I came to read the place I live as, in the words of cultural landscape historian J.B. Jackson, a "field of perpetual conflict." I wanted a situated poetics, a making that accommodates other-than-human needs too, that could ward off erasures of senses of habitability, that would create a document to help rescale our thinking about 21st-century inhabitance. This felt pressing, given what we know, and don't, of biodiversity extinction, habitat loss, and extreme weather events. We draw sustenance and identity from our landscapes, but places as we know them are changing. How do we begin to reexamine and reinvent our modes of inhabitance? This is a book for this place, a document of opening up human being and attention to the multiple and thinking along with these in time, which is imagination.

attention + imagination

The Author

Linda Russo lives in the Columbia River Watershed, tends garden plots and a blog (inhabitorypoetics.blogspot.com), and teaches at Washington State University. *Meaning to Go to the Origin in Some Way* is her second full-length collection of poems; a third, *The Enhanced Immediacy of the Everyday* (Chax Press), and a collection of lyric essays, *To Think of Her Writing Awash in Light*, selected by John D'Agata as the winner of Subito Press inaugural lyric essay / creative nonfiction prize, are forthcoming.

CPSIA information can be obtained
at www.ICGtesting.com
Printed in the USA
FSOW01n1257040816
23448FS

9 781848 613935